AMAZING INSECTS and SPIDERS

By George C. McGavin

WEEKLY READER®
PUBLISHING

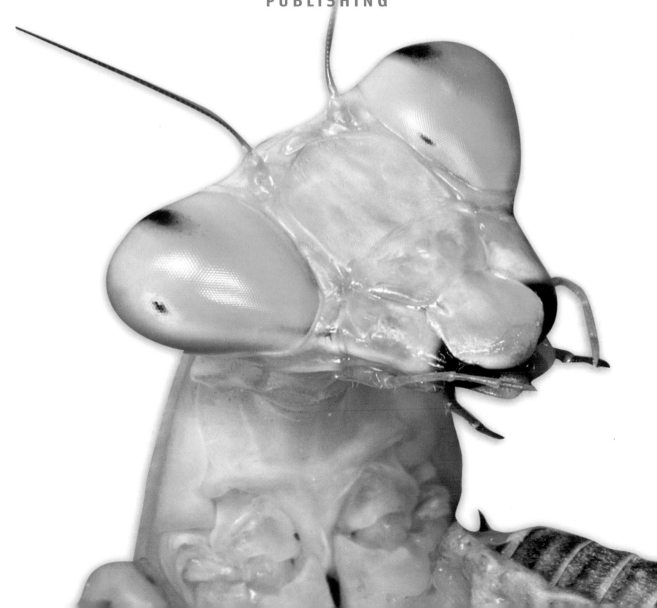

Please visit our web site at www.weeklyreader.com.
For a free catalog describing our list of high-quality books, call 1-800-542-2595 (USA)
or 1-800-387-3178 (Canada). Our fax: 1-877-542-2596

Library of Congress Cataloging-in-Publication Data

ISBN: 978-1-60626-004-3 (paperback)

This edition published especially for Books are Fun, a Reader's Digest Company.

North American edition first published in 2008 by
Gareth Stevens Publishing
A Weekly Reader® Company
1 Reader's Digest Road
Pleasantville, NY 10570-7000 USA

U.S. edition copyright © 2008 by Gareth Stevens, Inc. Original edition copyright © 2007 by ticktock Media Ltd.
First published in Great Britain in 2007 by ticktock Media Ltd., Unit 2, Orchard Business Centre, North Farm Road,
Tunbridge Wells, Kent, TN2 3XF United Kingdom

ticktock Project Editor: Ruth Owen
ticktock Project Designer: Sara Greasley
With thanks to: Trudi Webb, Sally Morgan, and Elizabeth Wiggans

Gareth Stevens Senior Editor: Brian Fitzgerald
Gareth Stevens Creative Director: Lisa Donovan
Gareth Stevens Graphic Designer: Alex Davis
With thanks to: Mark Sachner

Photo credits (t = top; b = bottom; c = center; l = left; r = right):
FLPA: 14cl, 16 both, 17t, 21tr, 21br, 24 both, 25, 28 main, 29. Nature Picture Library: 7cl, 7r, 11b, 15cl, 22c, 22b, 27t, 30b.
NHPA: 11t, 27b. Shutterstock: cover, title page, contents page, 4 both, 5 all, 6 both, 7t, 8 both, 9 both, 10 both, 11cr, 12tl,
13 all, 14tl, 14ct, 14b, 15t, 15cr, 15c, 15bl, 15br, 17b, 18 both, 19 both, 20tl, 20–21 main, 22tl, 23, 26 both, 28tl, 30tl, 31
both. ticktock image archive: map page 12, 14cr.

Printed in China

1 2 3 4 5 6 7 8 9 10 09 08 07

Contents

Words in the glossary appear in **bold type** the first time they are used in the text.

What Is an Insect?

Insects can be tiny, like an ant, or big, like this giant grasshopper.

An insect is an animal that has six legs. An insect's body is divided into three parts: the head, **thorax**, and **abdomen**. Insects do not have backbones. They are **invertebrates**. Bees, butterflies, ants, and beetles are all insects.

Insects have a pair of feelers, called **antennae**, on their heads.

Antenna

Leg

Head

Thorax

Insects use their antennae to smell, touch, and find out what is going on around them.

This close-up photo of an ant shows its main body parts.

Abdomen

AMAZING INSECT FACT
There are about 1 million types of insects on Earth. That is more than all other types of animals combined.

A dragonfly

Many insects, such as dragonflies, have two pairs of wings. Others have just one pair. Some insects have no wings at all.

A fly has one pair of wings.

A flea has no wings.

The eye of a fly is made up of hundreds of tiny six-sided sections.

Insects have compound eyes. Their eyes are made up of many small light-gathering sections.

Insect Life

Some insects eat only plants. Others hunt and eat other insects. Wasps, bees, and butterflies are attracted to brightly colored flowers. The insects drink a sweet juice that the flower produces called **nectar**.

Butterflies have a tongue. They use it like a straw to sip nectar.

Many insects eat dead wood from rotting trees. The **larvae**, or young, of stag beetles eat rotting wood.

Adult stag beetle

Some insects, such as ants, live in big groups called colonies. Others, such as adult stag beetles, live alone. Adult males and females get together to **mate**.

A firefly

Female moths produce smells that attract mates. After mating, the female moth lays a lot of eggs. She then leaves the eggs to **hatch** on their own.

A ruby tiger moth lays eggs on a leaf.

Some insects, such as aphids, give birth to live young.

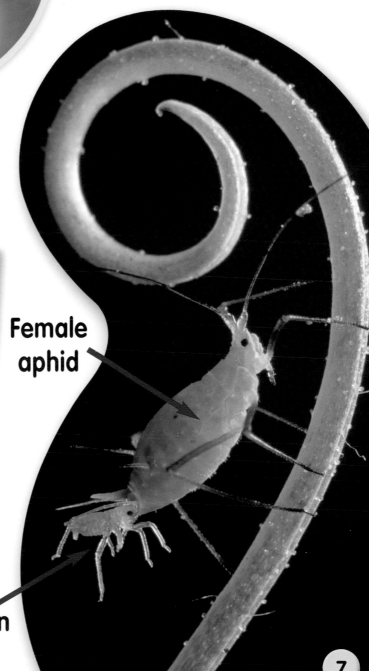

Female aphid

Newborn aphid

What Is a Spider?

Spiders belong to an animal group called **arachnids** (ah-RAK-nidz). All spiders have eight legs and two main body sections. Spiders are **predators**. They hunt and eat other animals for food.

Tarantulas are large, hairy spiders. They use some of the hairs to sense food and predators.

Leg

The spider's abdomen contains its digestive organs. It also holds special body parts, called glands, that make silk for building webs.

The spider's head and thorax are joined. This front part of its body is called the **prosoma**.

Prosoma

Abdomen

Palps

Spiders have two small limbs called **palps**. They use the palps for feeling and smelling.

Some spiders build webs. They weave their webs out of silk threads. The threads come out of a part of the spider's body called a **spinneret**.

Web

Orb web spider

Eyes

AMAZING SPIDER FACT
Most spiders have eight eyes. All spiders have fangs for injecting poison into their **prey**.

This jumping spider is holding a fly with its fangs.

Spider Life

Spider silk is thin but also very strong!

There are about 35,000 different types of spiders. Webs are a good sign that spiders are around. Webs made by orb web spiders can be found on plants, on fences, and inside buildings.

Some spiders sit in the middle of the web ready for prey to arrive.

Other spiders hide and wait. When their web begins to shake, they know an insect has become trapped in it.

Once its prey is trapped in the web, a spider wraps its victim in silk.

AMAZING SPIDER FACT
Spider silk is liquid until it comes out of the spinneret.

A trap-door spider approaches its burrow.

Trap-door spiders make underground **burrows** with a "door" covering the entrance. When the spider feels something moving close to the door, it jumps out and pulls its prey down into the hole.

Burrow

Trapdoor

Eggs

Adult spiders live on their own. Males and females get together only to mate. After mating, the female spider lays many eggs and wraps them with silk.

Many female spiders leave their eggs. When the eggs hatch, baby spiders, called spiderlings, must take care of themselves.

A nursery web spider carries her eggs with her in a silk egg sac.

Egg sac

Animal Habitats

A **habitat** is the place where a plant or an animal lives. Insects live everywhere from hot deserts to cold mountains. Spiders live in many habitats, too, but not in very cold places, such as Antarctica and the Arctic.

Up to 2,000 different insects might live in a single garden.

Insects and spiders live in most habitats around the world.

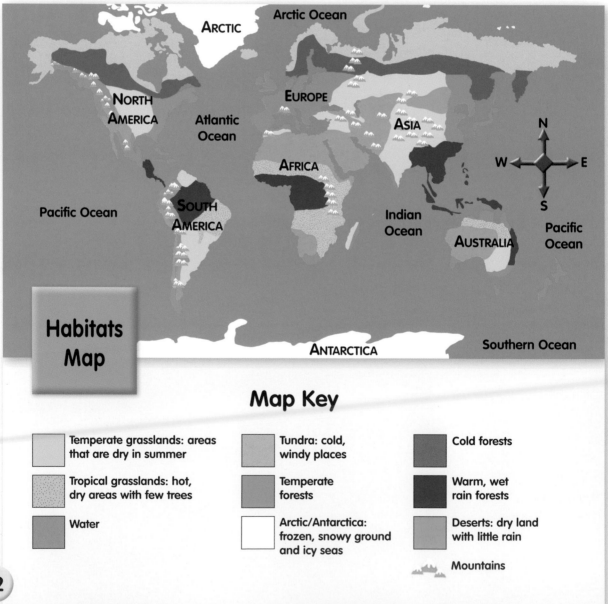

Habitats Map

ARCTIC

Arctic Ocean

NORTH AMERICA

Atlantic Ocean

EUROPE

ASIA

AFRICA

N

W   E

S

Pacific Ocean

SOUTH AMERICA

Indian Ocean

AUSTRALIA

Pacific Ocean

ANTARCTICA

Southern Ocean

Map Key

Temperate grasslands: areas that are dry in summer	Tundra: cold, windy places
Tropical grasslands: hot, dry areas with few trees	Temperate forests
Water	Arctic/Antarctica: frozen, snowy ground and icy seas

Cold forests
Warm, wet rain forests
Deserts: dry land with little rain
Mountains

Dragonflies and many other insects live in or near freshwater pools, rivers, and lakes.

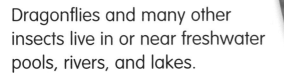

Dragonflies live near ponds and streams.

Leaf-cutter ants live in South American rain forests.

Leaf-cutter ants cut leaves and bring them back to the nest. The ants then grow a **fungus** on the leaves and eat the fungus.

Hundreds of different types of insects can live on a single oak tree!

What Is a Life Cycle?

A **life cycle** is the different stages that an animal or a plant goes through in its life. The diagrams on these pages show the life cycles of some insects and spiders.

Sometimes a female spider thinks a male in her web is prey, and she eats him!

1 A male and female meet and mate.

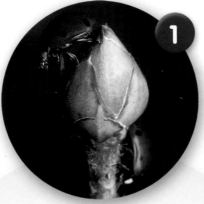

LADYBUG LIFE CYCLE
Many insects have a life cycle with these stages.

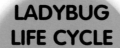

2 The female ladybug lays her eggs. She doesn't look after the eggs or the babies once they hatch.

4 Inside its case, the larva grows into an adult ladybug. The ladybug shown here has just climbed out of its pupal case.

3 A larva hatches from each egg. The larva feeds on aphids. The larva then makes a hard case around its body. The larva becomes a pupa.

1 An adult male and female meet and mate.

SPIDER LIFE CYCLE
Many spiders have a life cycle with these stages.

2 The female lays her eggs in a silk egg sac. Some spiders guard their eggs. Others leave them.

4 When the spiderlings' hard outer skin becomes too small, it falls off. They have new skin underneath. Spiders shed their skin four or five times before they are fully grown.

3 The spiderlings hatch. Some make a tangled web. The spiderlings grow bigger.

Amazing Insect and Spider Life Cycles

Praying mantis

Jumping spider

In the pages that follow, we will learn about the life cycles of some amazing animals—from praying mantises to jumping spiders.

A swarm of desert locusts can include 50 billion insects.

Locust

A swarm of locusts can eat a huge field of wheat in minutes! In a single day, a swarm of desert locusts can eat four times as much food as all the people living in New York City can eat.

After mating, a female locust pushes her body deep into the soil. She lays 100 eggs, one after the other. Female insects lay their eggs through a tube called an **ovipositor**.

Ovipositor

AMAZING INSECT FACT
Female locusts make a foamy substance that protects their eggs.

Foam

Eggs

Tiny locust larvae called nymphs hatch from the eggs.

Nymph

Large groups of nymphs are called bands. As they march along, bands eat all the plants in their path.

As the nymphs grow, their skin becomes too tight. It splits and drops off to expose the new skin underneath. This is called **molting**.

After they have molted five times, the young nymphs become adults with wings.

Adult locust

Wing

Praying mantises
have triangular
heads.

Praying Mantis

Praying mantises live in warm places where there are plenty of plants. They have very good eyesight and spiny front legs that snap shut on their prey.

Large eye

Front leg

It's easy to see how praying mantises got their name. They rest with their front legs held together as if they were praying.

A giant Asian mantis stalks a cricket.

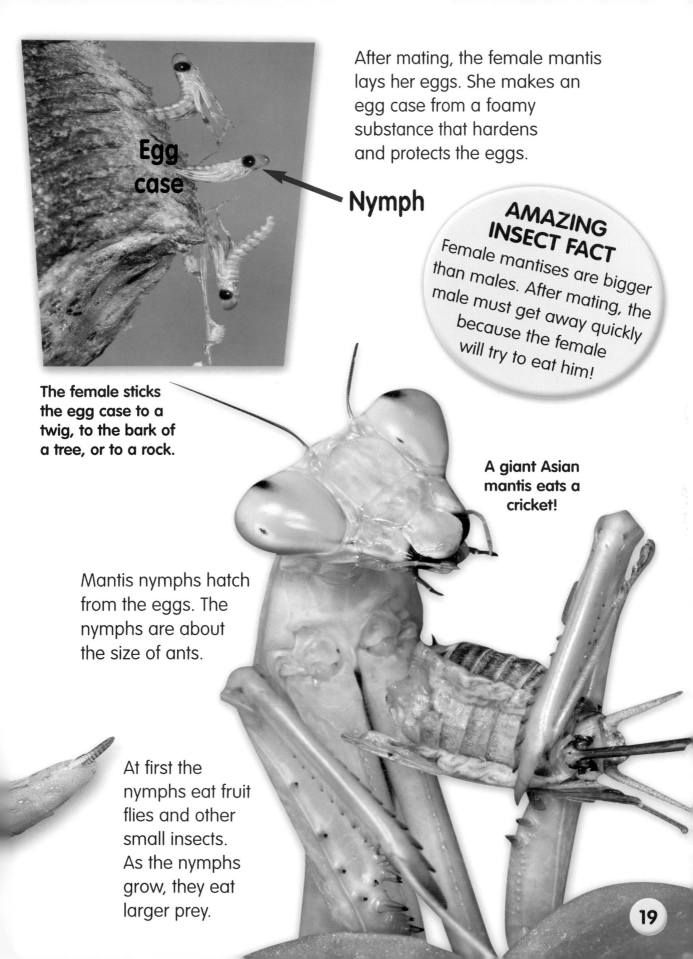

Egg case

Nymph

After mating, the female mantis lays her eggs. She makes an egg case from a foamy substance that hardens and protects the eggs.

The female sticks the egg case to a twig, to the bark of a tree, or to a rock.

A giant Asian mantis eats a cricket!

Mantis nymphs hatch from the eggs. The nymphs are about the size of ants.

At first the nymphs eat fruit flies and other small insects. As the nymphs grow, they eat larger prey.

19

Only the male rhino
beetle has a horn.

Rhinoceros Beetle

The rhinoceros, or rhino, beetle lives in rain forests. This beetle gets its name from its horn, which looks like a rhino's horn!

The rhino beetle is 2 inches (5 centimeters) long.

AMAZING INSECT FACT
Adult rhino beetles feed on nectar, rotting fruit, and sap from trees and plants.

Male rhino beetles use their horns to fight over territory with other males. If the male has a good territory with plenty of food, he will be able to attract a female.

After mating, the female rhino beetle lays her eggs. The eggs hatch into larvae. After two to three years, each larva becomes a **pupa**.

Rhino beetle larvae eat rotting wood and dead leaves.

Pupa

Inside its pupal case, the pupa turns into an adult rhino beetle. This change takes four to six weeks.

All butterflies have two pairs of wings.

Birdwing Butterfly

Butterflies live in many different habitats—from rain forests to city gardens. There are about 17,000 types of butterflies in the world. The Queen Alexandra birdwing is the world's largest butterfly.

The male and female Queen Alexandra birdwing butterfly look different from each other. The female is bigger than the male.

The female birdwing butterfly's wingspan is 11 inches (28 cm).

This butterfly's wingspan is bigger than the wingspan of some birds!

Male

Female

All butterflies have the same kind of life cycle.

A male and a female butterfly meet and mate. The female lays lots of eggs. Larvae, called caterpillars, hatch from the eggs. They eat and eat.

This is a monarch butterfly caterpillar.

The caterpillar gets too big for its skin. The old skin falls off and exposes a new skin underneath. The caterpillar molts several times.

Then the caterpillar makes a case around its body and enters the pupal stage.

Pupa

Inside the pupal case, the caterpillar becomes a butterfly!

This monarch butterfly is crawling out of its case.

Spider Wasp

There are about 4,000 different types of spider wasps in the world. The female wasp taps the ground with her antennae in order to find spiders.

When the female wasp catches a spider, she fights with the spider and stings it. The spider is paralyzed by the stinger's poison. The spider is still alive, but it cannot move.

A spider wasp sting can be very painful to humans.

Antenna

Wings

Wolf spider

The paralyzed spider cannot escape!

Burrow

The wasp then drags the spider to a burrow she has dug and pulls the spider underground.

AMAZING INSECT FACT

Some types of spider wasps are nearly 3 inches (7.5 cm) long. Most types are less than 1 inch (2.5 cm) long.

The female lays a single egg on the spider and then seals the burrow. When the egg hatches, the young wasp larva feeds on the spider, which is still alive!

The wasp larva spins a silk case called a **cocoon**. Inside the cocoon, the larva becomes an adult wasp. The new adult wasp crawls to the surface and escapes from the burrow.

25

Most jumping spiders
have hairy bodies.

Jumping Spider

Jumping spiders live in many habitats around the world, including forests and other wooded areas. There are about 5,000 different types of jumping spiders.

Jumping spiders have eight eyes. Two of the eyes look like car headlights. The spider's big eyes help it spot its insect prey and judge the distance of its jump.

Jumping spiders jump to catch prey and to escape from birds and other predators.

As the jumping spider leaps toward its prey, it leaves a safety line of silk behind. If the spider misses its landing spot, it can climb back to its starting spot.

Silk safety line

Hoverfly

AMAZING SPIDER FACT
The jumping spider can leap up to 25 times the length of its own body!

After mating, the female jumping spider lays many eggs at one time. She wraps the eggs in an egg sac made of silk thread.

This female has hidden her egg sac in a dead leaf.

The female guards her eggs until the spiderlings hatch.

Large water spiders eat baby fish and tadpoles.

Diving Bell Spider

The diving bell spider lives underwater in ponds or slow-flowing rivers. The spider creates a structure of silk that looks like a bubble. The spider fills its "diving bell" with air and lives inside the bell!

The spider sits inside the diving bell. When prey, such as an insect, passes by, the spider rushes out. The spider grabs the prey and takes it back to the bell to eat.

The spider sits with just its front legs dangling in the water. The spider keeps its head in the bell so it can breathe.

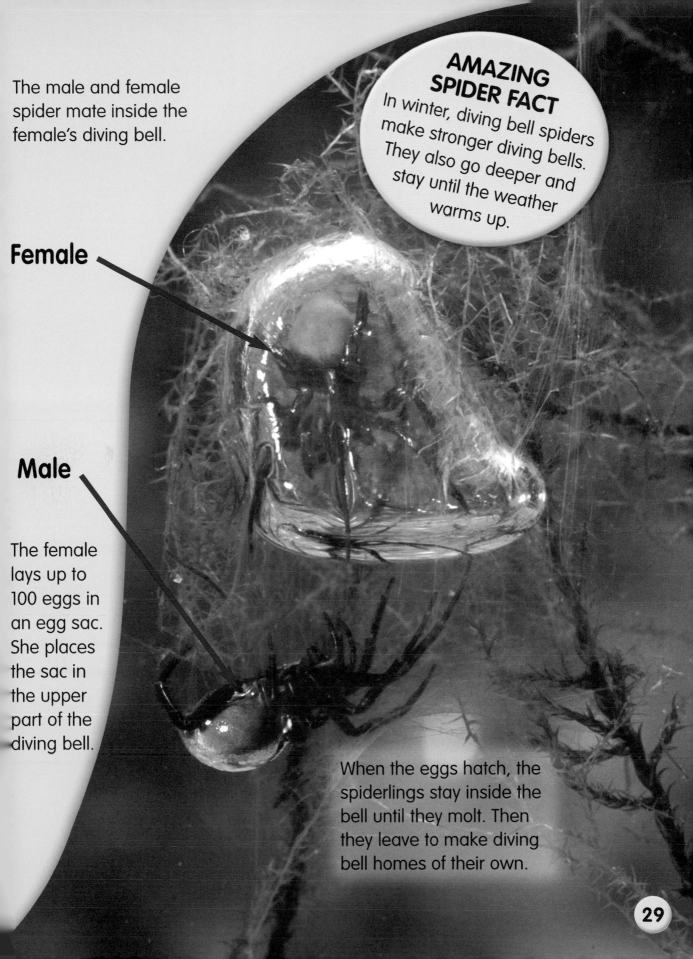

The male and female spider mate inside the female's diving bell.

Female

Male

The female lays up to 100 eggs in an egg sac. She places the sac in the upper part of the diving bell.

AMAZING SPIDER FACT
In winter, diving bell spiders make stronger diving bells. They also go deeper and stay until the weather warms up.

When the eggs hatch, the spiderlings stay inside the bell until they molt. Then they leave to make diving bell homes of their own.

That's Amazing!

Most insects and spiders do not care for their eggs or young, but some are amazing parents. These good moms feed their babies and protect them from being eaten by predators.

The female wolf spider carries her spiderlings on her back.

A female earwig cares for her eggs inside an underground burrow. She cleans them every day to keep fungus from growing on them.

Insects such as bees and wasps live in large groups. They make nests in which they look after their young.

Eggs

Earwig

Cell

Egg

Paper wasps make a nest out of chewed-up wood that looks like paper.

A female queen bee or wasp lays all the eggs in her group. She lays an egg in each cell of the nest. Larvae hatch from the eggs.

The other females in the group, called workers, help look after the nest and feed the larvae.

AMAZING INSECT FACT
Female paper wasps feed chewed-up insects to their larvae.

This paper wasp larva has grown into an adult. It is climbing out of its cell.

Glossary

abdomen: the part of an animal's body that contains the digestive organs

antennae: a pair of feelers on the heads of invertebrates, such as insects

arachnids: small animals with eight legs and two main body parts

burrows: underground tunnels and holes where some animals live

cocoon: a silk covering made by animals to protect their eggs

fungus: a simple living thing that grows and spreads, such as mold

habitat: the natural conditions in which a plant or an animal lives

hatch: to break out of an egg

invertebrates: animals that do not have a backbone

larvae: the young of some insects

life cycle: the series of changes that an animal or a plant goes through in its life

mate: to come together to make eggs or babies

molting: process in which an animal loses its outer covering (such as its skin or fur) and a new covering grows in

nectar: a sweet liquid inside flowers

ovipositor: a tube-like organ that female insects use to deposit their eggs

palps: small limbs near the mouths of invertebrates, such as spiders

predators: animals that hunt and kill other animals for food

prey: animals that are hunted by other animals as food

prosoma: the front part of an arachnid's body

pupa: an insect in the middle stage between larva and adult

spinneret: body part from which silk threads are passed

thorax: the middle of an insect's body

Index

TINA TUMBLES

Written by
Danielle Soucy Mills

Illustrated by
Kimberly Soderberg

To my mother, who instilled in me a lifelong love of reading, writing, and flipping. Without you, this book would not be. To my husband for his constant support—and to every kid who has ever dreamed a dream in their heart.
—D.S.M.

To Caroline, my role model and inspiration for Tina. I am lucky to have you in my life. Sky's the limit!
—K.S.

TINA TUMBLES
by Danielle Soucy Mills

Text copyright © 2014 by Danielle Soucy Mills
Illustrations copyright © 2014 by Kimberly Soderberg

Book design and illustrations by Kimberly Soderberg

FIRST EDITION
ISBN 978-0-9915338-6-2

daniellesoucymills.com

Nighttime arrived
and the stars lit up in the sky.

"It's time for bed!" Tina's mom cried.

But Tina did not feel tired.
Her eyes, round and wide,
focused on the T.V.
as she watched the gymnasts
flip across the screen.

Girls in shiny leotards
bounced high over the vault.

They swung quickly from bar to bar.
From the highest bar,
they turned somersaults.

They danced, twisted,
    and flipped some more
across a skinny balance beam,
        and all around the floor.
Every move looked so easy!

All of a sudden, the T.V. clicked off.
Tina's mom pointed to the stairs.

"Young lady, it is way past
your bedtime now," she said
with a glare.

Tina threw her hands to her hips.
She stomped her feet on the ground.

"I don't want to sleep," she announced with a frown.

Up the stairs Tina flew, jumping into her bed.

Instead of ducking under the covers,

she stood on her head.

"I want to try gymnastics myself," she said.

What an amazing sight it was,

the world upside-down.

But then...

Tina fell sideways onto the ground.

A loud banging sound echoed down the hall.

A headstand was not as easy as it seemed.

"Tina," her mom said,
"be careful please."

Tucking Tina in, she kissed her goodnight.
With the flick of a switch,
out went the light.

The next day was bright.
The sun sparkled through the clouds.

"It's time for breakfast!" Tina's mom called out.

But Tina was not hungry.
She wanted to try cartwheels across the couch.

Up went her legs.

Her body spun around...

Instead of landing on her feet,
she bounced onto her bottom.

"Ouch!"

Tina's mom rushed to her side.
She patted Tina on the head.

"Please be cautious, my little one.
Don't hurt yourself," she said.

But Tina wanted to try again and again.

Being upside down was just so much fun!

Soon it was afternoon.
The trees swayed in the breeze without a care.

"It's a warm, sunny day.
It's time for a walk," Tina's mom declared.

But Tina did not want to walk.

Letting go of her mother's hand, she bounded for the swing set. There were bars on both sides.

"I want to fly like the gymnasts on T.V. and the squirrels in the trees!" she cried.

So she tried and she tried...

But her legs flipped over her nose,

and she landed on her side

with a giant sigh.

Tina's mom picked her up and held her in her arms.
"It must be time for gymnastics class, my sweet pea."
This time, Tina agreed.

Tina's mom drove to Flyers Gymnastics.
Tina wore her very own shiny leotard.

With Coach Kim's help gymnastics would not be so hard.

Holding tight to her coach's hand,
Tina tiptoed across the high beam.

She nearly touched the sky
as she bounced
on the trampoline.

She jumped into the pit
piled high with soft foam.

There were so many things
she could never try at home.

Tina swung on the bars,
her coach guiding her feet to the mat.

Then she saw a girl
spinning cartwheels so fast.

"All by myself," Tina cried, "I want to try that!"

Without a thought or a worry
she threw her legs up
and then down.

Before she knew it, Tina tumbled over
onto the soft-matted ground.

"Hmph," Tina said.
She crossed her arms to her chest.
"I'll never, ever do it.
Every time I'll fall on my head."

"Don't be discouraged," Coach Kim said.
"All you need is practice,
and to always, always try your best."

Her best? Tina had a bad feeling,
but she held her arms up high.
She took a deep breath
and gave it another try.

"Kick your feet toward the ceiling," Coach Kim instructed. "Squeeze your muscles tight and point your toes. You'll land on your feet with corrections like those."

So Tina kicked up her feet to the ceiling and beyond.
She squeezed her muscles as tight as they would go.
As hard as she could, she pointed her toes.

Over she went and much to her surprise,
this time...

Tina landed on her feet, all on her own.

Picture Glossary of Basic Gymnastics Shapes

New to gymnastics? Here is a list of basic shapes that can be practiced at home to impress your coach at your first lesson. Already involved? Test your knowledge by going through each shape as fast as possible. You can also teach and test your friends. Please remember, before starting gymnastics each day it is important to warm up and stretch your muscles. The best place for gymnastics is in a facility with proper gymnastics equipment under the supervision of a trained professional. As Tina learns, gymnastics can be harder than it looks. Perfecting your basic shapes and skills helps to create proper gymnastics technique. It also makes progression of more difficult skills fast and efficient. Be safe and have fun!

Tuck   Pike   Straddle   Hollow

Tight arch   Knee scale   V-sit   Lunge

Bridge   Arabesque   Split   Candlestick

Relevé   Passé   Lever   Pushup position

Author Biography

Danielle Soucy Mills grew up in Massachusetts in a small city by the sea. Like Tina, she started gymnastics on the furniture in her home. She has since been involved with the sport for over 20 years, as a competitor and as a coach. At Rhode Island College, Danielle exercised both her writing and gymnastic abilities before moving to California to earn her graduate degree in Creative Writing from Chapman University. She lives with her husband and daughter in San Diego, where she enjoys writing books for children and adults.

Illustrator Biography

Kimberly Soderberg is a children's illustrator living in Cleveland, Ohio with her husband, Josh, her two sons, Wyatt and Grady, and her two dogs, Ralphie and Gertie. After graduating from the Columbus College of Art & Design with a B.F.A. in Illustration, her journey to becoming an illustrator in the children's book market began. Since then her work has been published in picture books, ebooks, coloring books and children's magazines.